Sprawl

Hollis Summers Poetry Prize

GENERAL EDITOR: SARAH GREEN

Named after the distinguished poet who taught for many years at Ohio University and made Athens, Ohio, the subject of many of his poems, this competition invites writers to submit unpublished collections of original poems. The competition is open to poets who have not published a book-length collection as well as to those who have.

Full and updated information is available on the Hollis Summers Poetry Prize web page: ohioswallow.com/poetry_prize.

Meredith Carson, *Infinite Morning*
Memye Curtis Tucker, *The Watchers*
V. Penelope Pelizzon, *Nostos*
Kwame Dawes, *Midland*
Allison Eir Jenks, *The Palace of Bones*
Robert B. Shaw, *Solving for X*
Dan Lechay, *The Quarry*
Joshua Mehigan, *The Optimist*
Jennifer Rose, *Hometown for an Hour*
Ann Hudson, *The Armillary Sphere*
Roger Sedarat, *Dear Regime: Letters to the Islamic Republic*
Jason Gray, *Photographing Eden*
Will Wells, *Unsettled Accounts*
Stephen Kampa, *Cracks in the Invisible*
Nick Norwood, *Gravel and Hawk*
Charles Hood, *South x South: Poems from Antarctica*
Alison Powell, *On the Desire to Levitate*
Shane Seely, *The Surface of the Lit World*
Michelle Y. Burke, *Animal Purpose*
Michael Shewmaker, *Penumbra*
Idris Anderson, *Doubtful Harbor*
Joseph J. Capista, *Intrusive Beauty*
Julie Hanson, *The Audible and the Evident*
Fleda Brown, *Flying through a Hole in the Storm*
Sara Henning, *Terra Incognita*
Andrew Collard, *Sprawl*

Sprawl

Poems

Andrew Collard

OHIO UNIVERSITY PRESS

ATHENS

Ohio University Press, Athens, Ohio 45701
ohioswallow.com
© 2023 by Ohio University Press
All rights reserved

To obtain permission to quote, reprint, or otherwise reproduce or distribute material
from Ohio University Press publications, please contact our rights and permissions
department at (740) 593-1154 or (740) 593-4536 (fax).

Printed in the United States of America
Ohio University Press books are printed on acid-free paper ∞ ™

Library of Congress Cataloging-in-Publication Data
Names: Collard, Andrew, 1987– author.
Title: Sprawl : poems / Andrew Collard.
Description: Athens : Ohio University Press, [2023] | Series: Hollis Summers poetry
  prize
Identifiers: LCCN 2022051168 (print) | LCCN 2022051169 (ebook) | ISBN
  9780821425282 (paperback) | ISBN 9780821448007 (pdf)
Subjects: LCSH: Detroit (Mich.)—Poetry. | LCGFT: Poetry.
Classification: LCC PS3603.O4387 S67 2023 (print) | LCC PS3603.O4387 (ebook) |
  DDC 811/.6—dc23/eng/20221130
LC record available at https://lccn.loc.gov/2022051168
LC ebook record available at https://lccn.loc.gov/2022051169

Contents

How to Be Held

Diorama

First, the remains of foil balloons littering the bank of the pond,
a string once tied to a child's wrist. Then, a pilot in uniform,

perhaps on leave, stepping quietly past the jungle gym and benches,
with his lover arm in arm. This is not a photograph, not a map. It isn't

landscape I'm after, but the way the pieces move, why a bomb
his father's squadron dropped in a field forty years ago, never cleared,

today undoes a farmer's face, returning it to carbon, iron, and air.
When the neighborhood I once mistook for home is placed in context

and stands revealed as hostile, the freeway south crowded with ghosts
of homes its engineers designed it to destroy, and when my child asks

what the letters stitched into my socks are spelling, as he runs his fingers
over each, and is rewarded with a brand name, the number of miles I pack

between the neighborhood and me turns trivial. I carry its history
inside me like a flu, exhale it every place I might escape to. I'm sorry,

but I have to build it, to construct the quiet of this park in summer, so you
can see it as construction. I have to call back every crumpled newspaper

beneath the overpass, and follow the avenue of offices and bars toward
the minor league ballpark, outfield sterile as a hospital floor, the thudding

of fireworks confused for jets or thunder every Friday night. I have to
reduce it all to this shoebox model, if only to understand its scale,

to guide you past the road signs, each bent slightly in a differing direction
by a stray car's bumper, to the one that reads *no outlet*, to the living room

beyond, where the steady creak of pipes, the water seeping, lulls
a man to sleep, and on the TV, tuned to breaking news, an explosion

rips across a darkened skyline, still frame veiled in wisps of smoke.

Future Ruins

Perpetual Motion

I drove. The Focus leapt. I slept inside a Civic

for four nights at a rest stop. East of Harper,

my whole existence packed into the trunk.

I rode. Like a witness, or misplaced luggage.

I threw up in the cabin of a duct-taped Cavalier.

Crown Vic. Astro van. Beetle. Blame it on

the road noise, or the radio. Smart-ass friends

who put me quick at ease. I shouted out the lyrics

of the MC5 from the back seat of a stranger's

Chrysler. Carried through the tributaries of the night,

toward . . . *what?* A bedroom's near-total stillness,

stray headlights through the blinds, solitude.

> When I wake
> to stillness, think of
> stillness, ambushed
>
> by how tenuous
> a thing it is
> to breathe, listening

as my neighbor's lamp or glass
bursts against
our shared wall,

I think of where
the crystal stillness leads
and whisper *I don't want to go.*

I circle back. Adrift in an age of endless leaving

as if home were not extraordinary. I called shotgun.

Bumped a cyclist. Watched my sister swigging whiskey

in her Cadillac, as she slurred unprompted questions

to the sky, the trees, the darkened houses. Ask me

where the day began, and I'll tell you everywhere,

or nowhere, how I steered an orphaned friend's Kia

up and down M-3, from Detroit into the sticks,

until he quieted,
then slouched
from his grieving

and into sleep,
while beside the car,
the ad-ridden fixtures

of the strip malls
and the churches blurred
into a path of light—

Quizzo Night at The Red Ox

Outside, a cruiser swims
               along the curb
      like a snake

that wants its hands back,
               the way the horde
      of snowflakes swim,

a million parachutes
               above the tavern.
      I watch my father,

in the corner booth,
               consoling me,
      age six, after the mower

that we pushed together
               swallowed up
      a nest of rabbits, some flung

to my sneakers, some
               into the bag—
      my father's fingers

resting on my neck, less
               grief than pity—
      and behind the bar,

my high school English teacher
               pours my ex
      a whiskey ginger

as the game begins.
                  To my left,
          the goldfish I won

from the parking-lot carnival
                  in sixth grade
          by targeting balloons

with darts—that didn't
                  make it home—
          remembers

the name of an actor
                  from *Full House,*
          a three-point answer.

To my right, my childhood dog,
                  the missionary child
          I once sent baseball cards,

and the fawn an SUV
                  in front of me
          decapitated on my birthday

smile awkwardly, asking
                  about the last book
          that I've read, and if

I've seen *The Wire* or
                  The Sopranos.
          I laugh so hard, I almost

forget the court fines
                  I've failed
          to pay, the warrant

and the way stray cops
                    run plates, the car—
            obscured—that always follows

from the corner of my eye.
                    It isn't
            the way my woozy steps

each land like boxes falling
                    from a truck, or
            the way my wedding ring

sits, preserved, behind
                    my bathroom mirror.
            It isn't resurrected bodies

that distress me, but
                    the bones
            inside them, waiting

to break skin, like red lights
                    in the rearview
            cloak the road.

Cicada Song

O the drag days the vertigo of earth   the sap the night the cruelty of jays
the mantises   the years I passed in darkness to elude them   winters
languishing above my head   O how many lives behind me now   the carapace
the bumbling climb the crater   the holes we leave   the city of tubers
subterranean   the sickened leaves the helicopters   O forgotten
weeks my father sang   above the world of men   trimmed branches
power cables sandbox song descending   to the empires of brick and mortar
the side yard the hose   the child demanding gulps the water
puddling in the grass around the halo of his muddy shoe   O harmony
the saw mower symphony of crickets   the percussive thudding
excavator dump truck traffic   whispering of the freeway love   O
can you hear me I am calling you   between the branches
the primordial maple the wellspring bark   the arm I sprang from O
the fall the sudden stop   the cushion of the world beneath me   O
the burrow and the boy who keeps watch from his window   O those years
the whole earth held me   the crusted husk the body I discarded
the frame I couldn't recognize still clinging   to the rotting deck
the old life crouched and pleading   to remain erect   to mother me   O
the blanket I would draw over the houses the ants   the daddy longlegs
wobbling in the dew   the rain the hose the shouting children   O
to tuck them in my love   O can you hear me heavy magic of the wing the sap
the chorus of the trees   the wild vibration echo chamber of my chest
the notes dispatched into the heat   the rushing water siren box-fan static
of the radio the womb my love   the space between the trees the sky
that cries *ascend ascend*   and all to find you all to know   I won't return

Pax Americana

(After David Hornibrook)

A hanging bulb swings   almost imperceptibly
in its own light, varying the shadows,   if barely, in the corners
of my uncle's empty kitchen after class.   No scent

       of butter melted   in the saucepan, no strayed shout intended
       for the TV and the ball game   being played mere miles
       behind it   through the wall, could make that sweatbox seem

any more inhabited   than others down the street,
each one the same: the carpets   immaculately clean, the quiet
scent of dryer sheets   meandering up the stairway,

       and stashed on the living room's   least conspicuous wall, a print
       of praying hands. In someone else's place,   every provision
       requires clearance, lying first beyond my reach,   and then

beyond my will, and twenty years will pass   before I learn
the sense of heaviness   this isolation brings me, this tenor
of a scar, in other tongues,   is known as loneliness.

       There's a distance, here, encoded   in the space between
       the houses, in the route   the cops take, circling the block,
       in the pixelated faces—the ones   who got away—

captured on the backs   of emptied cartons in the bin,
as though the neighborhood, itself,   were whispering *forget*.
Forget the nightly grate and whistle   of the 4:30 train,

its blue-coated conductors   so impatient for Chicago,
and the passengers   made faceless by their haste. Forget
the rails, those rusted bones   loosed from the flattened gravel

a thousand engines trusted   they would cling to, and the wires
still strung beside that track for miles   to either shore. Forget
the smokestacks towering   above them, spouting shrouds of steam,

the unsettled surface of the river,   and the peace
that hides beneath,   waiting to ascend, to lay this block
and all that its constructions might illuminate   to waste.

Autotopia

No longer the mail carriers,   the utility poles dispatching their charges
            to your every extremity, bearing the weight
of the signals that allow for your ascent,   no longer the skeleton built
            of backroads and freeways, cutting acres
of oak and the odd swamp,   the neighborhoods with their asphalt grids—
            O Autotopia, what will you bleed
once the wind becomes uncivil,   and the oil runs out? Will you spit
            in the face of the always-exploding sun?
Who will be left, then,   to unwrap the soft hands of broadcast
            from the foreheads of your million children
as they roll across the land, migrating daily   to their offices among the sky,
            to factories assembling cars or newspapers,
and then home, that their dwellings might somehow bless the earth, entrenched?
            Aren't they more like weather than a garden?
Aren't they more like wind   than what the wind blows over? I'm stumbling
            through the arboretum after dark, mosquitos
at my clavicles, or   breathing strangely at the wheel, as train lights flash
            and the gates jerk down and up and down, or
I'm scouring the clouded night sky,   from my bedroom window, for the source
            of whatever disturbance has awakened me at 3 a.m.
when suddenly, my forgotten impulse to leave   heaves through me like nausea
            or too much light. O how I wish someone
would look at me the way you do   the yards of new grass or chimney caps,
            as though I were some lute to be stolen,
that I might sing for them alone   a song to carry through your ecosystem
            of lust and smog. If I am where the dead things go,
I insist you send down one among your cast-out gods   to recover me,
            some Orpheus or other, whose fingers might
compel me out into the open evening   chasing down the notes he's wrung.

Future Ruins

Even the scrapyard's upscale now,

with its flag-spangled marquee, the husks of junked cars
barred off like a gated community
                    or the White House —
huddling before the newly christened *Innovation District's*
clutch of corporate offices, and Jet's Pizza.
                              Lately, M-59 and I

pass each other like strangers, hundred-thousand-dollar
monuments and signage posing
                    in the median like thirsty police
or a billboard sequence, rapt in praise of a mattress no one
is permitted to sleep on.

                    \\

                    Beside my Honda, cut scenes

of a hundred films wake suddenly into speech: here, the empty lot
where once my father's favorite bakery
                    slung rolls fraught
with cigarette smoke and cinnamon, nothing left now but a name
calling out from the aisles
                    of wholesale clubs and groceries,

and here, the Coney Island where my child used to cede our quarters
to prize pods every other month
                    in exchange for rubber dinosaurs

and sticky hands, which lately has renounced its heritage
to become another faceless Bar & Grill.

\\

Lately, I can't stop making lists,

as though exhaustive cataloging might explain, somehow,
what it means that I am from here
                              but can't afford a home here,
in the capital city of *controlled entrance*. Because to name
a thing can be a way to claim it,
                    I take as much as I can carry

and run, until the catalog overwhelms my capacity to shape
or make sense of the narrative:
                    Dawn Donuts, *debris*, Rock-a-Billy's,
debris, Farmer Jack, *debris*. Only Trinity Lutheran still persists,
the final vestige of old Hall Road—

\\

The thirty-five-foot-tall golden halo,

steel frame coated in aluminum, is wedged before Michigan's deadliest
intersection. It has no history,
                    pyrite glare obscuring border patrol
headquarters, Lakeside Mall, and a thousand offices that don't care
what populates them
                    any more than wrapping paper. Roadside,

two men with shovels maneuver a struck raccoon into a garbage bag
as cars approach, and swerve.

Whatever was here before
Target doesn't care. The drive trains of one hundred thousand
vehicles per day don't care.

\\

At the food court Magic Wok,

my son, fidgeting, knocks his cup of milk across the takeout box
I've bought for us to share.
                    While I dry the table, he goes to work
sopping up soaked rice and chicken, asks me *how much can we save?*
It's fifty years since Neil Armstrong
                              set foot on the moon, one hundred

since the advent of the assembly line, and a dozen mall birds
root under tables for garbage
                    meant for nests up in the skylights,
a shoot of grass stands through the cracked tile of the fountain
drained of water, and all of its lucky pennies.

Wartime, Rally's Drive-In

The neon sign blinks *soda*.
I, too, am arguing with the sun.
Stranded by a cracked timing belt
twenty miles out of town,
the tow truck come and gone.
Somewhere, coolant leaks
from a submerged power cable
into the straits of Mackinac.
A child is signed into the custody
of the state. The smell of exhaust
fills the cart-addled parking lot
of a grocery store too removed
from the idea of a neighborhood
to walk to. These are facts.
Plain as the suspicious gaze
of the cashier behind the window,
or the crackling of grease, the traffic
buzzing in the back of everybody's
brain. Heat vertigos the blacktop,
brick, the roadside gravel, and I am wet
to death, head cradled in my sweat-slick
arms, browbeaten. Somewhere,
a called-up soldier sips a Starbucks latte
across the table from her partner
one day before deployment. A flag
waits motionless on the lunar surface,
four hundred degrees hotter
than it was before daylight. I think,
I should eat something. I think, *I shouldn't.*
I think of how, this morning,

at the outpatient blood lab
where I pick up shifts, an infant screamed
with his whole body, notes drawn-out
as the nurse studied his feet,
the soles so covered in old bandages
she couldn't find a place to needle.

Carried

When I'm sick, I wish   whatever song is in my head
would stop. Tonight, it's the same   tune my mother sang
to tuck me in, its notes   the kind of kindness

        only distant trains still hit—soft   like a string
        of Christmas lights sort of   smiling from a darkened
        window—the same tune   I took up,

humming some, to steel myself   against the fruit-like
odor cloaking   my son's room—his sick bed, stuffed bear
and the bucket beside him—   too dull to be sweet,

        too thick to breathe. Some days, the house   seems crowded
        with intruders—   on the stairs, the countertops,
        and windowpane, all murmuring   a prelude to descent—

the days I walk   bags full of liquid to the curb, still body-
warm, so that the drips turn steam   before they hit
the filthy snow. Yet, when he reached   to take my hands—

        then cracked   from nervous washing—there was nothing
        more I wanted   than to hold him, and that old song
        was enough to soothe us, huddled there   and praying

that the angel would depart. Tonight,   there's no one here
except me, and that song   is stuck, rattling through
my enfeebled frame   like a fly caught in a screen, or

        some stray moisture   in a lung. Sometimes, when the melody
        dies down, a well-forgotten dream   or memory persists
        to take its place, the outline   of a church pew's

scuffed wood, enduring my mother's   nervous fingernails
and a child's thoughtless   graffiti—blue marker that won't
wash off, years after—while the preacher   asks

       O death, where is thy sting?   I used to think
       the price of dying   was detachment, a severing
       from what we gather   of the world—these flimsy

souvenirs—our songs, the memories   we don't want,
and the ones we do, the long nights   by my son's bed
almost whispering   *you are my sunshine,* while the wind

       rails inexplicably   against the window. I wonder
       if I get too sick, how will I know?   How will I make
       the hospital, unaccompanied   as I am—as everybody

comes to be, with time—if the fever   renders me
incapable of calling?   I don't know what my mother saw
before she went to sleep   the last time, but

       when I get sick—   and pray so hard for silence
       that I think   I might become it—I hear my boy
       begin to sing,   and then, become the song.

Clippings: Sterling Assembly Plant

(Chrysler Corporation, 1958)

Q: How did you make up your mind to become an engineer?

> *I guess I was naturally inquisitive about what makes things work—*
> *and I always wanted to know why they wouldn't.*

Q: How long did you work at the missile plant?

> *I worked there until I was drafted. I was in the mechanical lab.*
> *We ran tests on missile components.*

Q: What did you think of your job?

> *You never know what you'll be doing from one year to the next.*
> *It's brand new—missiles. They could branch out into anything.*

Q: What about the missile's nuclear capability?

> *As far as potential destruction is concerned, I have no reluctance.*
> *It's our job to be prepared.*

Q: Does your family ever ask about the missiles or the plant?

> *I never talk business at home.*

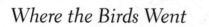

Where the Birds Went

Crawling Backwards

Once, you carved your name onto the steeple of your childhood church.
It calls to you as if you own it. Your prayers read like a list
of the space program's disasters. You're a curtain raised halfway.
A moth intent on catching fire here, in the backyard of the house
that you were born in. Where the spider hatchlings spill across
the window frame, and the cats are buried in an unmarked grave.
Where the guest room's nightlight is shaped like a crucifix.
The room you used to call your own. A room devoid of
Chatter Phones, Slinkies, and stuffed bears, replaced now by a shroud.
A place you can't remember what country your grandmother was born in,
only that it's somewhere hot, and that she's too dead now to tell you.
A place to start the map all over, to find out where the birds went.

The Nest

The nest is made of lint tufts and fragments of a Kit Kat wrapper, stuffed into a rotting corner of the porch's ceiling. Wind repels the approaching finch, plastic bag inflated from her beak like a parachute. I like to think the garbage pile amassing on the floorboards lives in service to her, a little less scavenging in the wetness of an opening world. Someone used to live here

> before the house fell into heaving silence: conversations
> turned serious, the birds flew startled from their coves.

I'd forgotten what it was to sleep alone, unfolding into spaces newly hollowed. First, books piled on the couch, the shelves slowly emptying; then flies infested the cat box, occasionally winding toward unwashed dishes in the kitchen sink.

> I like to think the nest is incomplete, as I read wrapped in blankets big
> enough to share. But socks left on the carpet speak like tea leaves:

> a mess of comfort built
> on remnants of another's
> home,

> and nothing's missing

> as outside, tulips open
> unobserved.

Unpunctuated Days

Despite my child up the hallway, breathing
so quietly the rhythm almost drags
all that surrounds him into dream, despite
my working through the late hours
while he slept under the almost-watchful eye
of his sleeping grandmother, despite
the weights behind each of my eyes, like stones,
that led me to collapse into position
on the couch, into the kind of stillness
dreams sometimes come to fill, my body has
rejected sleep, the fourth straight morning.
And in my clouded state, I had almost
managed to forget my pre-dawn
encounter at the front desk of the ER,
staring into the mouth of a man
whose lips, nearly severed in a wreck,
turned flaps of skin he held against his jaw
while trying to speak. But on returning
after 7 a.m. from my post recording names
and insurance cards to eat a necessary
bowl of cereal alone, there is no signal
that does not confront me with its passage:
the fuzz of my newborn's noise machine
pushing through the monitor, breaking news
of stock drops pushing through my phone,
the chorus of pinpricks pushing through
my arm as it goes numb, still sore from lifting
the boy into the air to distract him
from the teeth pushing through his gums.
Despite the absence of the throaty loon,

who yesterday cried inconsolably
for hours outside my window, unseen,
my body has rejected what it once
insisted on, and so I draw the curtains,
while in the parking lot, a gray-haired man
who's lost himself to dancing mimics
gestures, lifted from a video, in silence,
no speakers to relay the missing beat.

Elegy for the Dymaxion Car

(demonstration film, 1933)

00:05 [LOW-ANGLE SHOT]
Out of dust bowl, out of burden, Bucky Fuller's three-wheeled bullet pulses
toward the camera, imposing on the frame to obscure the crowd assembled
along the road to glimpse tomorrow:

\\

Zoomobile, he calls it, car-as-organism, wingless bird at war

with all that's not sustainable.   The body is a teardrop, a seed,

a submarine turned hitchhiker, rear wheel guiding twenty feet

of stock parts like a rudder.   My first thought is what it costs

to insure, then   if it might drain savings the way my Dodge

does, then   *but is it safe?* The body is a grasshopper, but

the engine is a Ford: at speed, I can almost mistake the blank

staring of its cabin for determination   as it throttles forward,

streamlined as a salmon. I can almost mistake its *spin and zip*

for something to believe in,   propelled by necessity from

the imagination to the once-abandoned auto factory to newsreels,

an assembly line of out-of-work mechanics   leading into sky.

For a moment all is shadow, passing under, earth abstracted into outline,
and what light leaks in thick as milk beneath the car's back end has only
come to swallow us:

\\

Freak Car Rolls Over—Killing Famous Driver,

the papers claim, as though   the aluminum had simply buckled,

Skidded—Turned Turtle, as though the organism tried

to shake off what had leashed it, there,   before the entrance

of the 1933 World's Fair. And just like that, the impulse toward

public relations sweeps in like a debt collector to claim payment,

the dream drooping back into its context, not much to thrill to.

Instead: interrogated, and explained,   the way I must explain,

when my son asks, that *heaven* is a story intended to assuage us,

scaffolding for what comes after. In the end, Fuller's prototype,

after a decade of advertising soda,   will be destroyed by fire.

Where are you now, Henry Ford? Where,   Walter Chrysler?

Postcollision, each appearance, with its attendant turn and bluster,

carries the air of spectacle,   cheapening *the future* to pulp—

It could waltz, Fuller says, *it really could dance very beautifully . . .*

The car passes over the camera like fitful sleep, and disappears into history,
bequeathing only dust and a far-off collage of treetops—crowd dispersed,
shadows dispersed, empty frame still perched against the gravel:

\\

It was never enough to eliminate distance, taxiing established

routes at record speeds, for less.   Even this could never

be sustained. *Dear daughter, dear dancer,* the Dymaxion vehicle

was meant to fly,   jump rough terrain, to make spot landings

sans runway, turbine-powered, and then settle back into traffic.

This is the long game: autonomy,   to be confined no longer

to profits, borders, short-term motives. Up the street, last week,

another child was struck while crossing at the signal. One lapse

in our attentiveness, and every future's futile, every question.

Roads don't *lead,* don't *meander* or *wind,*   cars don't *take* us

anywhere, or *run.* It's not about the cars, but how we end them,

how we end, stifled by the miracles   we've built to buy us time.

Autotopia

(Rochester Hills, MI)

I used to think it was a theme park   you were building,
       a haven detached from the rioting earth
to hold us: the components come by ship, some from
       complexes strung with suicide nets,
then by big rig,   to arrive here, where curated yards
       fill with gazebos, matching patio sets,
and marble Chihuahuas,   where even the Clinton River
       has begun collecting the discarded
carts and amplifiers.   I am tired of your dead-end visions,
       willful and incomplete, your countless
amusements that may outlive me.   Why is it
       the moments I feel most secure
are spent before a register?   At the Bean & Leaf, say,
       shelling out singles to refill my cup, or
the BP on the corner,   buying donuts with a Bridge Card,
       which I'm told, to prevent misuse,
the cashier must swipe himself.   This evening, I want
       to put my hand through the windowpane
of the nearest storefront   and make of it a memory, to push
       a cupped hand down its throat and pull
the stifled thrush out, breathing.   O Autotopia, how long
       will you allow me to loiter here, penniless,
among your children,   before your patience grows thin
       and you escort me from the premises?

They Say King's Forest Boulevard Is Healing

Have you heard about this house, its chimney sickened with rubble
and windows lit as if a place where something happened once

that now can only baffle passersby through a vernacular of creaking?
Floorboards loosed by damp and heel, it has no essence, no *where*,

but tell that to the tent worms stringing threads along the stoop,
or the branch they started in that someone must've trimmed away:

the question of their agency hangs over us and every other thing,
like an illness gone undiagnosed. Upstairs, a woman is scribbling

in her spiral notebook, eyes trained on a nearly empty glass of soda,
while in the alley below, a young man interrupts a stranger, spitting

through a haze of smoke and breath. We are each tucked in our separate
pockets of occurrence: night people, stalking the markets and lots,

our hands reduced to bone, night people blinking with panic in the dark
like scattered radio towers, asking *does anyone receive my signal*,

night people advancing and departing as the earth extends its jaws
to swallow us, our elegance and bad intention. We have no say in it,

this carousel of error, no stake in the pageant that has led us here.
Last Christmas Eve, the accrued news of an awful year went critical

along King's Forest Boulevard, and the sewer line beneath collapsed
into a football field's worth of sinkhole. We watched the crisis unfold

through the blinds, while finishing our chocolate cake and bean dip,
responders combing the buckled yards of reindeer. Twenty-three homes

evacuated, three condemned: chalk it up to sand infiltrating pipes,
the contractors who each descended through, and somehow overlooked

the one detail that could've answered everything. Do we blame them?
Tonight, I sit before the TV, indecisive, as the work of an effects team

begins to press on my attention like a phone that rings or doesn't,
the film replicating my experience of evening almost completely

in the way the space between the frames will soon become invisible,
while below my feet, the wooden slats, below the slats, concrete,

below the concrete: material deposits, gravel, the bedrock shale,
and a liquid core of iron, subject to tides, with its impossible burning

that sometimes rises to stand inside me in a shape resembling *human*.

Sub-pastoral

The syntax of the houses reads easy
                 and makes no sense, side yards
        and driveways built on what?

Origin's not a single point, untraceable,
                 but still the past slides forward
        populating all we don't consider

with itself. Somewhere there's a river,
                 then after millennia we come
        to know the river's history, piecemeal,

like a child knows the shapes of words
                 before their letters.
        The morning starts like this:

a type of tree, a type of grass, a father
                 in a vehicle, departing with
        a brand-name soda. A bouquet of fragments

intricately arranged to root us, those little
                 breathing things. But between?
        A man once told me spirit is

the name for what the living cast
                 that can't be caught, leaving
        patterns of silence, like the gaps

punctuating lineage, each no more important
                 than the last. The dandelions
        missing aren't a mystery, aren't missing,

aren't there nonetheless, opening from
                elsewhere, like broadcast, through
      the receiver of the body. A landscape's

nowhere but a point.to pin the storm on,
                a subdivision imposed, like a dream,
      by what's beneath it: the routes

worn into roads by the commuters,
                the envelopes addressed to no one
      living, yet delivered promptly

every day at three. What makes
                run-of-the-mill so alluring is
      all the death along the edges, the grasp

of what our comfort has required. It's like
                the blinds exist solely to gesture
      toward a sense of closure,

shielding a relief of jars, laundered shirts,
                and a child framed at the window,
      wondering if today will rain or shine.

After News of a Border Shutdown, I Venture Out for Fries

Can I interest anyone in the newspaper of my spirit? Feathers,
today, it's mostly feathers. Once again these field reports from the interior

    have failed to document the wildlife rattling around in me,

goings-on lost to the usual grammars of a Monday crowded
with anxious thoughts. Nevertheless, as the drive-thru line at Wendy's

    winds out from the parking lot, and drivers mug

to jockey for position, as fringe groups graffiti their invective
across the internet, and the border we once disregarded like robins do,

    day-tripping in our family van, is closed,

I riff toward some clause that might disrupt this arrangement
the world seems to be stranded by, mid-performance, grounding us inside

    our separate plots beneath the signal. If to love someone

is to devote to them my full attention, I am afraid that I am
losing the ability to love. If I flinch before the storm, bartering like a zealot

    at the steering wheel as rain begins to pummel bystanders,

I am no more likely to arrive at my intended destination
still intact. Perhaps it is you, Neil Young, disembodied and streaming

    through the speaker of my Ford, who will accept my confession:

my mother lived in America for twenty years before
she decided to become a citizen, and when she did, I skipped the ceremony,

    my distaste for posturing even as a teen too terrible

to swallow. I think now, beneath the blacklight of a war
that wouldn't end, what I mistook for flag-waving in the federal courthouse

    was for her an act of self-defense, *in medias res,*

the moment when she felt most threatened, reciting to the judge
his own secondhand pledge as the landscape inside her dimmed into memory

    and the birds there one by one began to lose their names.

Clippings: Sterling Assembly Plant

(Johnston Island, 1958)

At first, the explosion produced a bright flash, with a cloud beginning to
appear in its center. Later, concentric rings of color formed, and the cloud
slowly moved higher, spreading as it rose.

Witnesses reported that a red shell appeared to pass overhead about forty
minutes after detonation.

*

After the event, we observed
quite a few birds

sitting or hopping
on JI docks

in a helpless manner.
Either they had been blinded

or they were unable
to dive for fish,

their major food supply,
because the ethereal oils

which protect their feathers
from getting water soaked

had been boiled off
by the thermal pulse.

Sprawl

Gas & Food

Whose words are these,

refusals astonishing my tongue
              like broken teeth,
how many have I swallowed

            bad days, allowing the condemned
gas station up the block
         to be labeled *baggage*,

the way I have my debt-collection phone calls,
                  or divorce,
or my apartment's warping floor,

          where figurines and diaper boxes idle?

A sprawl this extensive breeds
            empty pockets, and silences
that someone will insist on filming,

             camera fixed to capture
what they call *collapse*. How horrible
             to be you, they say,

as though the La-Z-Boy left rotting
            on my neighbor's driveway
were code to be deciphered,

         and *hallelujah from the rubble*
the acceptable response. This is not
            the end of days, but Thursday:

this morning, I drove my child
                              to watch planes taxi at the airport
where no one on staff cares enough

                              to chase us off. At the supermarket,
Gala apples are on sale, again, each so swollen
                              they insist on being shared.

Whose words are these,
                    pushing through my chest like hurts,
so unfamiliar they must be pronounced

                    over and over, until they are understood?

Key Motor Mall

No postcard to preserve the raygun gothic angling of the roof

back in its prime, no scrap metal left to thieve. No plaque

to designate this structure, rounded like a child's idea of a spacecraft,

as historic site, no air of nostalgia, even, for the used Oldsmobiles

a representative once strong-armed local motorists into owning.

I am scavenging the emptied spaces to better understand myself,

what's running through me, drawn to sunburst, steel, and flair,

the exaggerated aesthetic that passersby dismiss as tacky, that I, too,

blew by every morning, barely looking, the same sleek shapes

and comic-strip bombast embellishing so many coffee shops.

Where are all the drivers, those production workers and cashiers

born, like me, a few miles off, sold a future their every shift enshrined

a little more as fiction? If the fallen-in ceiling and concrete walls

are extensions of the bodies that built them, the way breath is,

and the language breath carries, then what's discarded is discarded by design: the husks of factories or houses, the body no longer electric,

no longer strong. How, then, to become invisible, radiant as the memory

of neon, O stranger, which road will usher me at last toward the gates

of the atomic city? I am looking beyond the abandoned pumps

and walls of glass to somewhere *care* can be acquired. Somewhere else.

On the Demolition of Produce Kingdom

It's not just the violence required, or the adrenaline spike
stemming from my triggered impulse toward self-preservation,
that leaves me in a state of awe before the collapsing structure,

but the irrevocable change made to a landscape suddenly
so unfamiliar, how this simple grocery's disappearance orphans
the overcompensating neon of Pete's Coney and the blank

stare of Rite Aid into space, as though the composition that I name
the neighborhood has had its milieu removed, the crowd gathered
by the bus stop left uprooted. It's not about the innumerable

instants of awakening, among the crates of shapely avocados or
the smell of bread, to the simplicity of what sustains me, it's not
about the evenings salvaged wandering the aisles, unaccompanied,

but about my sense of order, how the makeup of the block,
assumed as constant, is used to track what manifests and dissipates
across it, each epoch sealing in its cars, clothes, and passersby

mid-revision, another way I have of feeling held. The chronology
I'm left with is a reinforcement of my own self-myth: I can pinpoint,
in my memory, the year my parents' neighbor swerved and wounded

fatally our mailbox, with its sticker reading *no scab papers*, because
the tallest maple in the yard still stood, then, before the blast
of wind it couldn't weather. I used to watch those maples

thrashing through the dark hours from my window, every shiver
immense enough to move a child to prayer, and in the aftermath
at daybreak, they'd resume their quiet bearing of the calendar—

almost peering through the rain-pocked glass—each as old as anything
I've known, as the discovery of penicillin, or the atom bomb,
a history encoded in their flesh that fastens them to earth,

each taking debris and yet debris itself, losing limbs without regard
for anything but holding on. They loom, as giants do, enough
to get forgotten: dig one up, and the ground beneath goes loose.

Telway Lament

1.

And then one morning,   just before the sunlight turns to bees
at my bedroom window, I will see it,   through fog—

a half-smoked cigarette   flattened on concrete, or the rippling
of a cruddy puddle—some image I will chew   through afternoon,

until the shadow burgeoning above me   dissipates, like an acquittal.
And I'll remember, then,   how home is gathered, and walk

awhile, before I grow too frail   and start to eat myself away,
the way a memory gets whittled   to a single detail

and nothing more,   the way each too-bright morning has become
this single too-bright morning—   the same old *brand new day*

my mind's been peddling   for months—and every evening taxed
by lonesomeness becomes another reason   I should leave. Some nights,

I want nothing more   than to insert this bad year in the middle
of some better era, to go back · somewhere I will know myself as settled:

I can't be caught up   in another movie, can't bring myself to cook
or sleep, and so I pull my boots on,   and take a drive—waste gas,

wear the paint-chipped body out—until   the embers snuff, or
until the light burns low enough   it goes unnoticed in the dark.

2.
And what place isn't meant   for passing through? I think,
the smell of grilled onions radiating   above the bar.

Gray-haired men   line up on stools like sunflowers
droop in too-hot August, shooting shit   as if they'd grown here,

and in truth, they have,   congregating three nights every week
since the 1980s. They come to be with people   and they come

to be alone, each enduring memories   of some private *golden age*
they hope to resurrect,   if only for a few hours, as each fry,

slider, and chocolate shake   does its mouth-to-mouth on whatever
cherished moment   the chemicals and lightning in their minds

half-conjure. This is what I mean   when I tell you *I remember*:
a kind of faith   in an abandoned language, a way the landscape

has of naming me—the way I once mistook   a marigold, an aster,
and a black-eyed Susan   for a garden, roadside—when my bedroom

ceiling bares its blunted teeth   past midnight. The only miracle I know
is isolation: a man in a Tigers cap squints   to recognize me,

standing at the glass door, but I don't live here   anymore, and never
learned to say goodbye,   like a regiment that goes on fighting

days after the war is lost. Some nights,   relief is like a squad car
stumbling on a tipsy driver. Some nights, I drive home   on empty

and fall to bed   faceless as a scratched LP—needle skipping—
carrying the probing glances of the passerby   into my sleep,

as though the contours of my body   had forgotten me, the way faith's
fortitude is drawn   from disavowal of the mystery it sprang from.

3.

Call it faith, call it garden—call it home,   if you want to—call it
nothing: to hunger, to return, and to be filled. Perhaps I lie in bed

all morning, and watch a common spider,   hidden badly
against the chipped paint above me,   no web to speak of—

how long has it been there?—until my hunger   pushes me to stand,
and, sensing movement,   the spider flees. Perhaps my son wakes early,

asks for yogurt—clapping   his hand against his chest, the sign
for *please*—and I carry him toward the fridge.   Across town, a man

dressed in frayed jeans   tells the grill cook he just made twenty dollars
raking leaves, and that he feels rich   as a senator, carrying his coffee

out into the wind. To engage, to surrender: and what more, he thinks,
could earthlings want?   Sliders. Caffeine. Fries at any hour of the day.

Autotopia

(Royal Oak, MI)

The signal drifts in from a paint-chipped Dodge on Twelve Mile
where a bundled-up girl begs her father to wait with her

until the school bus arrives, and from the father's impatience,
implying his child has, this once, become a burden,

and from the school itself, two miles off, where they've armed
the monitors and teaching staff at last. Autotopia, you hail me

from the shelves of the hypermarkets, the courthouse statuary
with its wrought-iron riffs on *conquest,* and the arena downtown

where bodies slap against each other on the Sabbath, shouts
erasing our attempts at speech. Even the gas station I frequent

for awful coffee, and the deserted body shop next door,
the scattered equipment too large to scrap, even the spaces

by now existing only in my memory, dissipating like steam
above a paper cup, O Autotopia, even these are safely tucked

behind the shield of your foreign interventions and profits —
the Malibus you've planted like radio towers across Shenzhen,

Rio de Janeiro, and Perth relay your gospel of estrangement
beyond every horizon, steel pockets to be paid off and insured

insisting we all make it into work on time each morning.

Badlands Flashback

We woke blank as though   we'd been born there,
at the end of praise, no ode
 persisting to anything,   among trails of eroded rock,

off-white, that we walked despite the glare
of whatever past refused us,   surrounded by
   a shortgrass thick with rattling. Our every

footstep resounded   like a burst of comm static,
unsettling the heavy air. Beyond us,   the state highway,
          two lanes through desert,

could've been Colorado or Dakota,   the painted booth
          cars queued before
   to buy passes   denoting the entrance

to Four Corners, or Yosemite.   I can't trick myself
     into remembering it any better,
can no longer locate us   by the type of wildlife

dead   on the roadside, or
     the orange barrels lined up like birthday candles
on certain routes.   What I know

      is we left
to look for god   or his replacement, and ended up
impatient for arrival, as if   distance itself

might be disposable,   like a grease-stained wrapper
     that once swaddled fries,   as if
 we could each, as lovers,   divorce ourselves

from the process of our bodies—
      the old mistake   of presuming movement
had the power to erase   the taste of emptiness

hanging in our mouths.   What I know
      is I am moving, again,   toward confronting
what my body has become to you,   which parts of me

have become someone else's   as we dissipate
      into our components, the minerals,   or deposits,
whatever it is they say   this flesh and blood is made of.

Night Music

Without the sound of shots fired up the block, like a conversation
             between blown-out tires, and crickets swelling up

    to mask the dead air after, without the flashlights of police

grazing the windows, and voices relayed in from neighbors' yards,
             what blessing for this hurtling earth would we have left

    to offer, what would our attempts at praise be worth?

Here, the calendar's been emptied of its saints, and when the tape runs out,
             the click of the recorder cutting off is all the solace we'll receive.

    There is nothing any less holy about the bombed-out house

next door than there is a cornfield, or the names we give the grass.
             There is no worldly space that wouldn't rather shun us,

    with our frenetic dreaming, our baby monitors, and drawn blinds.

Long after the street goes back to sleep, the motion sensor floodlight
             beside the house continues flickering on and off, to signal yes,

    it, too, is becoming restless, and yes, I should begin to map

our exit, just in case. O false god of *solitude*, may the luxury of standing still
             be, again, afforded to your most unlikely angels: tonight,

    all I believe in is the constellation of toy trucks neglecting

to take cover across the kitchen. Holy is the half-emptied box of Cocoa Puffs,
        the glinting of the tea kettle, and the backpack slung from

    a wooden chair. Holy is the silence of the fruit fly as it winds

up the hallway, the soft breath of the A/C wafting it toward the bedroom,
        and the child dozing there, so spent he must be eased

    awake in time for breakfast, long after the day's first bus departs.

Commute

(The Detroit Newspaper Strike, 1996)

Shrove Tuesday, I watched them through the windshield
of my mother's Astro van, kneading palms together
before the plant on Metro Parkway, in order to incite

the necessary heat to lift morale. Such commotion
I had yet to witness, except perhaps inside a church: as if
a parade had broken out, but slowly lost its impulse

in the dark hours of the morning, the cold air rendering
each breath as an escape. I was reading *X-Men* then, or
at least absorbing panels, I recognized the heavy coats,

the shouts, the cavalcade of strangers massed in service
to a conflict that I couldn't grasp. Some marched, hand-stapled
posters raised toward the avenue — *Honk If You're With Us* —

at 7 a.m., others gathered around the barrels rife with fire
inherited from other days. *We are not safe*, they seemed to say,
you are not safe, as though my mother's box of glass and steel,

built for hurtling, was all that held me, those few inch-thin layers
of wrought earth. And then the stoplight changed, and OOF
the congregation vanished in the sideview mirror, and POW

my mother scared up the city's final box of pączki, and ZAP
the ancient line of school buses parted: in the end, I wasn't
even late for class. Bleary-eyed, the picket would continue

deep into tomorrow's ashes, and for another year beyond,
its lingering questions cast off to the courts, all distantly
removed from those subfreezing interludes, the bodies

that were then so tangible. *We are still here*, they assured us
from the roadside, from the fading stickers on our mailboxes
and our parents' bumpers. I am still here, navigating signals

and crumbling infrastructure, bracing for another year's
impression of dire weather from someone else's Dodge,
dear neighbor: we are not safe. Honk if you're with us.

Clippings: Sterling Assembly Plant

(Chrysler Corporation, 1958)

Q: What's the future for Detroit in the missile business?

> *We think it is a growing continuous operation. It could go a long way in stabilizing the employment situation here.*

Q: What about the operation in Alabama?

> *Well, other areas of the country are selling us short. They're running us down in the race for space-age business. But Detroit doesn't have to take a back seat to anybody.*

Q: What's it like inside the plant?

> *There are two million square feet of floor space and over eleven thousand people—engineers, technicians, management, and production. They all seem to take a high degree of professional pride in what they do.*

Q: What might the Army do if the walkout is not halted?

> *If the strike continues, it will definitely have a serious effect on the missile program. The Army may seek new fields.*

Q: And if the program is discontinued?

> *Practically everyone here will be out of work.*

How to Be Held

Church can be a word for anywhere

an alley you skipped work to smoke in, a public fountain
you sat before, begging yourself to change, or
any of the innumerable landscapes in whose grasp you were opened,
made helpless by new light.
                              And love, if these moments are enough
to bless a space so unremarkable as the room where I was born
before an audience of technicians and fluorescence, or
the location where I will one day cease to exist,
                                        then why not
the front seat of the Honda Civic I fell into every morning
near-oblivious to the sun's ambush of Orion, to the layer of dust
coating the dash like a light snow, the cup holders filled with portraits
of politicians, etched in copper,
                              and the caked sugar of jostled Cokes.
Why not the deep-blue frame, the cracked windshield I returned to
after long days informing patients of their rights, families desperate
for relief, or diagnosis, or for leaving,
                              the thumb-worn steering wheel
I returned to, again, after dark, as though for an hour of prayer,
to hit the Tubby's drive-thru, or CVS for aloe, to circle the block
awash in my own unspeakable and solemn feelings amid the thudding
of *Purple Rain* or *Germfree Adolescents*, burning scraps of the past
to get from here to here
                              until the days stretched into a single day,
and the transmission finally gave out on a block riddled
with unretrieved mail jutting out of boxes, with upended sidewalks,
spoiled food, and rumors of human bodies.
                              I must return, again, to the scent
of air-conditioning fluid as it slowly leaks into the cabin, to the creak
of brake pads worn too thin, to the wheels passed down like an apology

back before this state of constant crisis found me, before I stopped
calling it a crisis.
               This time, come with me: we'll tour the ruin,
even if the motor sounds like shit, or takes a couple tries to fire.
See? Here is the food counter where Neil Young once jotted lyrics
on a napkin, stranded by a broken van. Here is the overpass we idled by
while the storm engulfed it with debris. Here is the house we thought
was ours to lose, here is the garden—
                      how we lost it is nothing new.

Landscape with Ryegrass and Hunger

That we know what is important and true can't save us
         from the lingering suspicion
there's something here the tyranny of image can't account for,

         tucked between stones
in the unpaved driveway, the slats of fences, and beneath,
         where theoretically the roots

of oaks reach down through layers of deposit. This afternoon,
         I poured a bowl of cereal
and scribbled to myself reminders like *emails for O & B*

         and *which province of Spain,*
entrusting to a sticky note each fragment in defense
         against its disappearing,

just before the sound of some catastrophe arrived outside:
         a blast out by the highway, maybe,
puncturing the present tense, or a semitruck reversing

         into brick, calling every neighbor
to their window, to reassure themselves the block has not
         been shelled. What facts we have can't

pledge us their allegiance, and in the absence of a siren
         to confirm the worst has happened,
we must navigate the distance between danger and our bodies

         by sifting through its echoes, before
the incident is filed away, a confusion several people had
         in common once. If there's a motif

the painters might wish to devote their paint to, it's the stoop
                after stoop jutting out through
bushes, a scheme of interruption mimicked everywhere

                along the network of side streets:
you can see it in the way occasional fenders turn the walk
                impassable, and stray hoses coil

horribly over blades of ryegrass more idyllic in their fading,
                these routines a stranger
could take comfort in, although the details tell us

                less and less. Imagine how many
headlines we'll never make, at home in our troubled context,
                where already the kids return

to powering Big Wheels over obstacle and stunt, where
                porches have begun to fill again,
and mostly, we will amble back into our yards and doorways

                without a sense of urgency,
even as the hour ages into hunger, and in the exosphere
                above us, the night goes on and on—

Idyll

Because anyone could've been a bullet, any backfiring van
punctuating the hum of traffic like a performance artist;

　　　because the private places, too, were spoiled by inspections,

and roaches in the cracks of the stove, fridge rigged
with receivers; because one touch from you and sand began

　　　to fill my shoes, my chest, and one touch was enough

to kill the process tree, rife with spyware, my thinking
had become, we ran for cover like school kids, mid-drill,

　　　like fireworks reflected in a skyscraper we've not been in,

which, one day, will be reduced to dust. Because we were afraid
our love songs, too, would self-destruct, this is how

　　　we never happened: in a meadow behind a megachurch,

with stalks of grass irritating our palms and ankles, the incline
working against us in every way, and inexplicably brimming

　　　with grown-over railroad tracks that surfaced, like wildflowers,

for meters at a stretch, like crab grass, nascent afternoons
that never once have asked for our devotion, returning only

　　　after-hours, between the lines, the most unlikely places.

City of Windows

From this one, driver's side,

we can see the traveling carnival has cast its garbage
to the vacant lot by Shamrock Pub
                              while big rigs and commuters spew
exhaust through the corridors of Thursday evening. It's always
like this, someone's debris swallowed
                              in a deluge of new debris—

From this one, in a tower above the city, the sweep of the grid
sprawled at dusk, before us, is so great
                              as to be almost unbearable,
a dim labyrinth of cul-de-sacs and driveways along the outskirts,
staggered like fires up a hillside.

\\

                              From your kitchen, where an insurgency

of dough puffs like an eye prepared to weep, we can almost, at a distance,
make the stuffed bear, strung
                              off the nearest streetlight, and the carnations
scattered to the curb beneath it, in memoriam. At any moment
we are trying to remember
                              have I brushed my teeth today, or

how soon must I buy another box of tissues, as if we had invented
the idea of time
                    just to make some sense of all the fragments,

these scenes that come to wear our bodies out like suits
into the malls, riverbanks, and hospice.

\\

So much of my happiness occurs

in spite of things that I've forgotten what it is to wake
to quiet light, the neighbor's TV,
                              and a dog vacating the bed because
what evening's left of you and me has found its way to singing.
This is new: our frames become one frame,
                                        and your bedroom window

another in the greater catalog of windows, in which
we're caught half-clothed
                              and wandering, indifferent to the gaze
of anyone who might be watching from the theater
of the darkened sidewalk—

\\

You ask me *did you see it, or did I?*

At the diner on Twelfth, a neon sign left burning after-hours
still signals *yes, we're open,*
                              as the reflection of an airplane bound
due east slips faintly along the bottom of the glass. It's not
that we are loitering
                        in that weathered booth for coffee after coffee,

but that we could be, it's not that I am scouring the landscape
for things to tell you,

but that I've come to love these glimpses
we are gifted, hurtling through, the excerpted strangeness
of the new familiar air.

\\

With your front door cracked,

by morning, we can watch the sprinklers switch back on
and the dog walker begin his route.
                              The comfort of this trivia
is that we are the trivia: we collect each particular like a postcard,
make a whole of them,
                    out of all their unintelligible fingerprints

and greetings. Behind our own reflections, from the city bus,
we can see the once-burned
                          house at the corner of Hill, rebuilt
so completely no one quite recalls the way it held itself, the windows
yet to be curtained, as if to say *come through*.

Night Cycle

This boxing match between tomorrow
and your will to sleep is set
in the space left
where the garage's door won't shut,
just wide enough for a rabbit
to push its quivering body through
and leave a skeleton
impeccably arranged on the concrete.
You found the whole brood by the fence
dead, wondered where the mother went.
To remember the shovel's heft
as you lifted little bodies to the bag
is to start mistaking bones for keys.
This time, be kinder. The empty space
in bed beside you isn't missing
anyone, the way statues seem taller
before they're named. The way
night asks *how far apart can bodies be*
to still be called a cluster
is not a sign the house needs selling.
Today your son pushed Matchbox cars
across the quiet floor, dashing to the window
to catch sight of a departing bus.
Do you still wish to be lifted,
wondering who could be so strong?
Remember what it is to look for something
and be caught breathless
when something better finds you,
the way a rolling glass will pause
at the table's edge, before it falls.

Autotopia

(Detroit, MI)

Today I descend the stairs of the old parking garage
as though I'm under anesthetic,
                    fragments of the past washing over me
until I am unable to name the artifice of your piazzas,
to call your smokestacks out as noise.
                      These gaps in memory
impose on my attention the way your various structures do
on the sprawl of the landscape
                    as your children leap between them
in their F-150s, Chevy vans, and discontinued Buicks, as the buses
and elevated train cars offload bodies
                    in exchange for other bodies.
Even so, I remember the gas station up the avenue, selling what passes
for New York–style pizza
                  spinning behind a pane of glass,
and the intersection it took a full ten minutes to navigate on foot,
how I was so sure, then,
                  of my father's command over the crowded street
I never questioned, never thought in all the world
we could be lost.
                We were going to the same place
all those grim travelers out along Jefferson were going, the place
they disappeared to,
                the traffic shooting west toward the Harbor Terminal,
with its warehouse painted a startling blue, the dock where the ferries
loaded passengers bound for Boblo
                and your cargo ships departed
filled with steel coils, wire, and slabs destined for auto plants.

We were going

        where the years went, as we watched entire decades
dissipate up and down these streets we walked, hand in hand,
the same place we're still going,

                in all the world no day like this.

To My Son Henry, Asleep in the Next Room

Where the Lane Closed sign sits flashing night and day
before the window of a stranger's house, this afternoon

we paused amid the smell of tar so you could watch the crews
repair the road, and as a Bobcat shoveled out excess soil,

I supposed, to myself, whoever lived there must have adjusted
to the constant lights and rumbling like an eye does to a scratch

across a lens, to see around it. Maybe the sounds of work,
after a while, become a kind of song to sleep by, like the ones

we sing at bedtime to muffle the passing cars, our too-loud
neighbors, or the imposed silence of evening. Tonight,

when our setlist of Beatles songs and lullabies ran dry, you asked
to *talk some mo'*, for me to tell you, again, about the time

I came across a train in flames in the desert night, every detail
witnessed from the window of my van, or about the highway

I used to drive in circles in your early days to calm you,
how I'd carry you gingerly through the doorway, up the stairs,

and to your crib, then sit in the next room over listening
through the monitor, in case you cried out. Even now, as you

lie sleeping through the wall, in the same room where you once
sweated out a fever under blankets, and against my shirt,

where the rocking chair shrieks some nights beneath me
like a key against a fence, and other nights is soundless,

I'm astonished at how awake I have become, at just how much
I can recall: the sidewalk of your first steps, upended

by the roots of maples. How you held to both my hands
and tumbled forward step by wobbly step, delighted in your own

ability to make great lengths of pavement disappear beneath you.
The way your eyes would drift, as we walked along the street,

toward the treetops, lost to the spell of the twisting branches,
and the way you reached out your hand as if to grasp them.

Dear leasing office, dear oil slick,

I did not come to curse this plot of earth,
brickwork bounce house   stricken
                           with resting bitch face,
or its Pandora's box of kid feet, continually thundering
back and forth on the fourth floor.
                           Dear long-emptied birdfeeder,

ghost, and broken screen,   this season's token cliffhanger
requires I pack my things and disperse
                              into a cold front of engine rips
and oh-shit brake wails, to let the asphalt eat my tires off
mile by mile. Where will I live, now,
                           with my heart made of shingles,

my faulty memory, and minivan,   trunk stuffed with shoes,
as I flounder toward home like a tune
                           pitched above my hearing?
Dear weather vane, white pine,   dear quick-fix drywall
heavy with questions,
                     in memory of complete strangers

knocking after midnight to inquire after a Wi-Fi password,
or a light,   or the whereabouts of a missing spouse,
                                          I have returned
to give this king-size calendar I spilled my days against
one last blessing before I go.
                     Let vines reach their fingers

across your every fence,   ascending the utility poles and power cables,
let the neighbors' wind chime

irritate the complex into dissonance.
Let the commons reek of garlic and burnt spatula, and the A/C units
stop, drop, or roll, midsummer.
                              May the parking-space vigilante

continue etching cuss words   on the doors of random cars
to fracture the mask of calm
                              swallowing these dubbed suburban yards,
and the phone grinding off and on against your shared wall
always expose as myth the notion
                              I have ever been alone.

Acknowledgments

My thanks to the editors of the following publications, in which many of the poems for *Sprawl* first appeared.

AGNI: "Sub-pastoral"

American Literary Review: "Pax Americana"

Bennington Review: "Wartime, Rally's Drive-In"

Best New Poets 2020: "Badlands Flashback"

Cincinnati Review: "Dear leasing office, dear oil slick" and "Gas & Food"

Diode: "To My Son Henry, Asleep in the Next Room"

Dunes Review: "The Nest"

Florida Review: "Autotopia" (Sterling Heights, MI)

The Journal: "Autotopia" (Rochester Hills, MI)

Juxtaprose: "Night Cycle"

Nashville Review: "*Church* can be a word for anywhere"

New Poetry from the Midwest 2019: "Carried" (reprint)

Normal School: "Telway Lament"

Ploughshares: "Carried"

RHINO: "On the Demolition of Produce Kingdom"

Salamander: "Diorama"

Sixth Finch: "Quizzo Night at The Red Ox"

Sonora Review: "Elegy for the Dymaxion Car"

Third Coast: "Key Motor Mall"

Thrush: "Cicada Song"

TriQuarterly: "After News of a Border Shutdown, I Venture Out for Fries" and "Night Music"

Virginia Quarterly Review: "Perpetual Motion"

Washington Square: "Unpunctuated Days"

Waxwing: "Autotopia" (Detroit, MI)

Witness: "Future Ruins" (winner of 2020 Witness Literary Award for
  Poetry)

My thanks also to the following people, without whom this book would not
exist: Deborah Augustin, Karalyn Bell, Henry Collard, Emily Daniel, Jacob
DeVoogd, Jennifer Kwon Dobbs, Nancy Eimers, Abigail Goodhart, Sarah
Green, Cody Greene, Dennis Hinrichsen, Edward Haworth Hoeppner,
David Hornibrook, Danielle Isaiah, Alyssa Jewell, Felicia Krol, Matt Morgan,
Sara Lupita Olivares, William Olsen, Olivia Olson, Lindsay Rhean, Cuba
Rhodes, Monica Rico, Isadora Savage, Miles Smith, Vanessa Stauffer, and
Connor Yeck.

Notes and Dedications

"Perpetual Motion" is dedicated to Dennis Hinrichsen.

"Pax Americana" is dedicated to David Hornibrook, and is an homage to his poem of the same name, which can be found in his book, *Night Manual*.

"Future Ruins" is titled after a song by Swervedriver.

"Clippings: Sterling Assembly Plant" refers to a factory, located in what is now Sterling Heights, MI, that was opened by Chrysler in 1953 to produce missiles capable of carrying nuclear warheads. Works cited:

Bellows, James. "Detroit Can Lead World in Missiles." *Detroit Free Press*, February 2, 1958.

"Chrysler Missile Adds 2,000 Jobs." *Detroit Free Press*, June 4, 1958.

Hoerlin, Herman. *United States High-Altitude Test Experiences: A Review Emphasizing the Impact on the Environment.* Los Alamos, NM: Los Alamos Scientific Laboratory, 1976.

Sudomier, William. "Outer Space Beckons to Young Engineer." *Detroit Free Press*, July 7, 1958.

Sudomier, William, and Dick Tripp. "Mass-Produced Death?" *Detroit Free Press*, January 29, 1959.

"Crawling Backwards" is dedicated to Matt Morgan.

"Telway Lament" references a chain of small hamburger stands in Metro Detroit. The location in question is in Madison Heights. This poem is dedicated to Felicia Krol.

"Badlands Flashback" is titled after a song by Bruce Cockburn.

"Elegy for the Dymaxion Car" references a prototype vehicle designed by R. Buckminster Fuller.

"City of Windows" is dedicated to Hoffa the dog.

"Autotopia (Detroit, MI)" references Boblo Island Amusement Park, which operated on an island in the Detroit River from 1898 to 1993.

"To My Son Henry, Asleep in the Next Room" is titled (almost) after a poem from Bob Kaufman's *Solitudes Crowded with Loneliness*.